The Real Deal

Drugs

Rachel Lynette

Heinemann Library
Chicago, Illinois

Designed by Richard Parker and Tinstar Design Ltd, www.tinstar.co.uk
Printed and bound in China by Leo Paper Group

12 11 10 09 08
10 9 8 7 6 5 4 3 2 1

Library of Congress Cataloging-in-Publication Data
Lynette, Rachel.
  Drugs / Rachel Lynette.
    p. cm. -- (The real deal)
  Includes bibliographical references and index.
  ISBN-13: 978-1-4034-9693-5 (hardcover : alk. paper)
  ISBN-10: 1-4034-9693-5 (hardcover : alk. paper)
  ISBN-13: 978-1-4034-9700-0 (pbk. : alk. paper)
  ISBN-10: 1-4034-9700-1 (pbk. : alk. paper)
  1. Drug abuse--Juvenile literature. I. Title.
  HV5809.5.L957 2007
  613.8--dc22

                              2007014734

Acknowledgments
The publishers would like to thank the following for permission to reproduce photographs: Bubbles/John Powell p. **12**; Corbis/LWA-Dann Tardi p. **4**; Corbis Sygma/Alan Lewis p. **19**; Getty Images pp. **20** (Matt Cardy), **21** (Taxi/David Oliver), **24** (The Image Bank/Ghislain & Marie David de Lossy), **27** (Taxi/Chris Sanders); Masterfile/Jeremy Maude p. **15**; Photofusion/Melanie Friend p. **23**; PhotoLibrary.com/Bill Bachmann Photography p. **26**; Rex Features pp. **5** (Marja Airio), **11** (SAKKI), **13**; Science Photo Library pp. **6**, **7** (Adam Hart-Davis), **8** (Robert Brook), **9** (TEK Image), **10** (Gustoimages), **17** (Cordelia Molloy), **18** (Gustoimages), **25** (Deep Light Productions); SuperStock/Lisette Le Bon p. **22**.

Cover photograph of an arrow road sign reproduced with permission of iStockphoto/Nicholas Belton; cover photograph of a syringe reproduced with permission of Getty Images/PhotoDisc; cover photograph of pills and capsules reproduced with permission of Corbis.

Every effort has been made to contact copyright holders of any material reproduced in this book. Any omissions will be rectified in subsequent printings if notice is given to the publishers.

The publishers would like to thank Kate Madden for her help in the preparation of this book.

Disclaimer
All the Internet addresses (URLs) given in this book were valid at the time of going to press. However, due to the dynamic nature of the Internet, some addresses may have changed, or sites may have changed or ceased to exist since publication. While the author and publishers regret any inconvenience this may cause readers, no responsibility for any such changes can be accepted by either the author or the publishers.

Contents

Some words are shown in bold, **like this**. You can find out what they mean by looking in the glossary.

What Are Drugs?

A drug is a substance that changes the way a person's mind or body works. Drugs can change the way a person feels, thinks, and behaves. Drugs can help a person who is sick, but they can also cause serious damage and even death if they are not used correctly. There are many kinds of drugs, and people take drugs for many different reasons.

Many people take drugs when they are sick or injured. People can purchase **over-the-counter drugs** such as cough syrup and aspirin at drug stores and most grocery stores. When people have a more serious illness or injury, they may need to use a drug that is prescribed by a doctor. Over-the-counter and **prescription drugs** can help people with their medical conditions, but it is important to use these drugs as directed. When these drugs are used inappropriately, they can be harmful.

Prescription drugs should be used only under the care of a doctor.

People use many kinds
of drugs recreationally.

Top Tips

It is important to use and
store drugs safely. Here are
some drug safety tips from
the Food and Drug
Administration (FDA):

- Always take drugs
  as directed.
- Never take someone
  else's medicine.
- Tell an adult right away if
  you think the medicine is
  making you feel sick.
- Store all medicines in their
  original, labeled containers.
- Store medicines where
  children cannot get them
  and use child-resistant caps.
- Throw away outdated
  medicines.

Recreational drug use

Some people use drugs
recreationally. Recreational
drug use involves using **illegal**
drugs or using over-the-counter
or prescribed drugs in ways
not directed. People use drugs
recreationally because they like
the way the drugs make them feel.
Recreational drug use is not only
illegal, but it is also dangerous
and often **addictive**. The only way
to use drugs safely is to use them
under the care of a doctor or other
responsible adult.

Types of Drugs

There are many different kinds of drugs. Most of the drugs that people use recreationally fall into one of the seven categories explored in this chapter. Illegal drugs are sometimes called street drugs.

Marijuana

Dried leaves and flowers from the hemp plant are used to make **marijuana.** People who use marijuana usually smoke it. Marijuana is sometimes called pot, grass, weed, reefer, or herb. Marijuana gives the user a mild feeling of **euphoria,** and it is addictive for some people. It can also be a **gateway drug.** This means that people who use marijuana are more likely to go on to use stronger drugs.

Case Study

Ethan started using marijuana when he was 13 years old. At first it was just on the weekends with friends, but soon he started smoking it every day. Smoking marijuana became the most important thing in Ethan's life. He felt sick, irritable, and depressed on days when he could not get any.

Marijuana comes from the hemp plant. Its leaves are easily recognizable.

In some states it is legal for people to use marijuana to treat certain medical conditions such as cancer and **glaucoma**, an eye disease. Marijuana is illegal for recreational use in all 50 states.

Depressants

Drugs called **depressants** make the user feel relaxed. They make the body work more slowly. They may also make a person feel drowsy. Most depressants are used for treating **anxiety** and sleep disorders. They are legal when they are prescribed by a doctor. Depressants include Valium, Xanax, and tranquilizers. Sometimes they are called downers, barbs, or ludes. Depressants are dangerous when used recreationally and can be addictive. Alcohol is also a depressant.

NEWSFLASH

Xanax is one of the most popular prescription drugs that teenagers abuse. At a middle school in Philadelphia, several students were taken to the hospital after taking Xanax pills. The pills were brought to school by a 13-year-old who had taken them from a relative.

Many depressants, such as Valium, come in the form of pills.

Inhalants

Common household products that give off fumes can be used as **inhalants.** These include correction fluid, nail polish remover, and model glue. There are more than 1,000 different kinds of inhalants. When their fumes are inhaled, they cause a feeling of euphoria. This is called sniffing or huffing. Whippets, poppers, snappers, and rush are street names for inhalants.

Inhalants are extremely dangerous to use. They can cause permanent damage to the brain or to other parts of the body. They are also extremely addictive. They can even cause immediate death. **Sudden sniffing death** can occur any time a person uses inhalants.

Common household products can cause serious harm and even death when they are used as inhalants.

NEWSFLASH

Studies have shown that parents can decrease the chances that their children will use drugs just by talking about them. Unfortunately, many parents either do not know what inhalants are or do not understand that they are dangerous. As a result, they may not talk to their kids about them.

Hallucinogens

Drugs that cause **hallucinations** are known as **hallucinogens.** These drugs cause severe behavioral, mood, and personality changes. Hallucinogens include LSD, PCP, and some kinds of mushrooms. They may be called acid, angel dust, or shrooms. Most hallucinogens are illegal. Hallucinogens are usually taken by mouth.

Although hallucinogens are not addictive, they can have very negative side effects. A user may have a "bad trip." This means that his or her experience might involve frightening hallucinations and intense feelings of panic, anxiety, or depression. During bad trips, people might try to hurt themselves or others.

People who have used LSD may also experience **flashbacks.** A flashback is when someone experiences the same sensation they felt when using the drug long after the effects of the drug have worn off. Flashbacks can occur weeks, months, or even years after the last use of the drug. In addition, using hallucinogens can cause permanent brain damage.

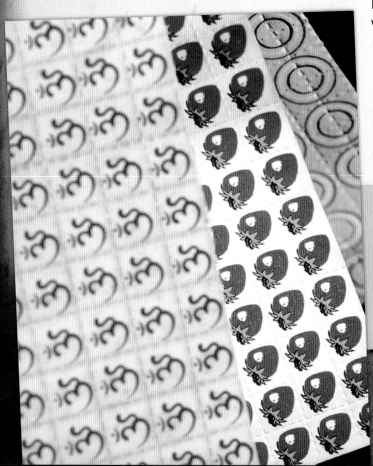

These colorful squares may look harmless, but each one contains a dose of LSD.

Stimulants

Stimulants make the body work faster. They increase alertness and energy, and can give the user a feeling of euphoria. Uppers, speed, crack, meth, and X are street names for stimulants. Some stimulants are prescribed by doctors to treat medical conditions. For example, people with Attention Deficit Hyperactivity Disorder (ADHD) may have trouble focusing and concentrating. Stimulants can help them. Stimulants are also used to treat obesity. These drugs are legal when used as directed.

Crack, cocaine, methamphetamine, and MDMA (Ecstasy) are illegal stimulants. Stimulants are often used recreationally and are very dangerous. Stimulants can cause violent behavior, **paranoia,** and anxiety. They can cause permanent harm to the body and the brain. In addition, stimulants are highly addictive.

NEWSFLASH

Kids with ADHD are often prescribed the stimulant Ritalin to help them stay calm and focused. But some kids sell their Ritalin pills for illegal use. Schools and parents need to make sure that prescription drugs are taken only by the kids to whom they are prescribed.

Cocaine is usually snorted through the nose, while crack is most commonly heated and smoked.

People who use heroin usually inject it directly into the bloodstream.

Narcotics

Doctors prescribe **narcotics** to help relieve pain. Narcotics can also give the user a feeling of euphoria. Narcotics include OxyContin, Vicodin, morphine, and heroin. They are sometimes called horse, smack, OC, oxy, or vic. Narcotics are extremely dangerous when used recreationally, and are highly addictive. Heroin is one of the most addictive drugs in existence.

Anabolic steroids

People take **anabolic steroids** in order to increase body mass and build muscle. Some steroids are legal for medical purposes. However, some people take steroids illegally to enhance their athletic performance or appearance. Anabolic steroids can be called roids, gym candy, stackers, or pumpers.

Using steroids can be very dangerous, especially for young people. Steroids can permanently stunt growth. They can cause cancer, kidney damage, high blood pressure, high cholesterol, and severe acne. They may also cause extreme mood swings, aggression, and depression.

Why Do People Use Drugs?

People use drugs for many different reasons. Most people use over-the-counter drugs for minor medical problems. They use drugs prescribed by their doctors for more serious medical conditions. Even though it is illegal, people of all ages use drugs recreationally. Most recreational drug users are teenagers and young adults.

Most people start using recreational drugs because they enjoy the "high" drugs give them. The drugs may create feelings of euphoria, energy, or relaxation. But people often do not realize that the drugs they are using are dangerous and addictive.

Many teenagers start using drugs because of **peer pressure.** They may think that using drugs will help them fit in with people that they want to be their friends. They may be afraid that they will be made fun of or rejected if they do not take drugs. Teenagers who give in to peer pressure and use drugs are breaking the law. They are putting their health and maybe even their lives at risk.

Peer pressure is often a factor in recreational drug use among teenagers.

Studies have found that some kinds of antidrug ads may actually increase drug use. This is because rather than making teenagers think about the dangers of using drugs, the ads make them curious. Ads that work best focus on the positive aspects of not using drugs.

Singer Justin Timberlake has admitted to using recreational drugs.

Celebrity drug abuse

Teenagers are influenced by people they admire. When they hear about celebrities using drugs, they may want to use them, too. Singer Justin Timberlake surprised and disappointed his fans when he admitted that he has used drugs. Darryl Strawberry, a baseball player, has a history of drug abuse that has resulted in multiple arrests, jail time, and several league suspensions. In 2005, supermodel Kate Moss was filmed using cocaine. Her drug abuse cost her several modeling contracts. Some celebrities, such as actor River Phoenix, have died from drug **overdoses.**

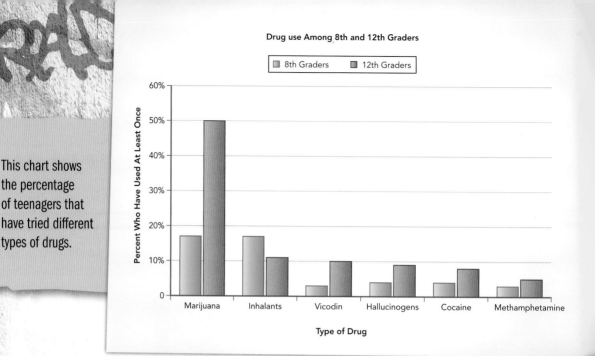

Drug use Among 8th and 12th Graders

■ 8th Graders ■ 12th Graders

Percent Who Have Used At Least Once

Type of Drug

(Marijuana, Inhalants, Vicodin, Hallucinogens, Cocaine, Methamphetamine)

This chart shows the percentage of teenagers that have tried different types of drugs.

Popular drugs

Marijuana is the most frequently used illegal drug. It is also the first illegal drug that many young people try. About half of all high-school seniors have tried marijuana.

Inhalants are popular with younger teenagers because they are inexpensive and easy to obtain. One in six eighth graders has tried inhalants. Although it is legal to purchase the products that are commonly used as inhalants, people who inhale them are not using them appropriately. Many states have laws regulating how these products can be used.

Recently, the number of teenagers abusing over-the-counter and prescription drugs has increased. One in five high-school students has admitted to experimenting with prescription drugs. Often, teenagers get these drugs from their own homes. Using prescription drugs inappropriately is dangerous and illegal.

NEWSFLASH

A recent study found that more teenagers today are abusing prescription and over-the-counter drugs rather than illegal drugs. One reason for this is that many teenagers mistakenly believe that prescription drugs are safer and less addictive than illegal drugs.

Case Study

Mitchell was 17 when he was arrested for selling a small amount of marijuana to an undercover cop. He did not know that there was a preschool in the basement of a church nearby. Mitchell was charged with selling drugs in a school zone and sentenced to two years in prison.

Drugs and the law

Recreational drug use is illegal in all 50 states. Every year thousands of people are arrested for using, possessing, and selling illegal drugs. People who are caught with drugs may be subject to community service, fines, and jail time. Penalties are harsher for those who sell drugs or who are caught with large amounts of drugs. Penalties are also higher for using or selling illegal drugs in a school zone.

Selling and using recreational drugs is against the law.

How Do Drugs Affect People?

A drug's effect depends on many factors, including the kind of drug, how much was taken, the way it was taken, and the user's unique body chemistry. Drugs can be swallowed, smoked, inhaled, or injected. No matter how drugs are taken, they always end up in the bloodstream and are carried to every organ in the body, including the brain.

Short-term effects

Drugs work by changing the way the brain makes or uses chemicals. The chemical changes in the brain affect the way the person thinks and feels. Drugs also affect the way the body works. Some drugs speed up heart rate and increase alertness, while others slow the heart and cause relaxation.

What do you think?

Some schools require drug tests for participation in sports and other activities. Supporters say that the tests keep kids from using drugs and help identify kids who need help. Opponents say that the tests are not always accurate and can give parents a false sense of security. Do you think schools should test kids for drugs?

Drugs can be taken in different ways.

Drug	Street Names	How Taken
Marijuana	pot, grass, weed, reefer, herb	Smoked or eaten
Inhalants	whippets, poppers, snappers, rush	Inhaled
Amphetamines	speed, uppers, dexies, bennies	Swallowed, inhaled, or injected
Methamphetamine	meth, crank, crystal, glass, ice	Smoked, swallowed, or injected
Depressants	downers, barbs, ludes	Swallowed
Cocaine	coke, snow, blow, nose candy	Inhaled
Crack	freebase, rock	Smoked
LSD	acid, blotter, microdots	Licked or swallowed
MDMA	ecstasy, XTC, E, love drug	Swallowed
Heroin	smack, horse, junk	Injected, smoked, or inhaled
Steroids	juice, roids, gym candy, stackers, pumpers	Swallowed or injected

People who are high on marijuana will feel a mild feeling of euphoria and may have trouble thinking clearly. They may not be able to finish a sentence because they forget what they are talking about. **Coordination** can also be impaired, and heart rate increases.

Inhalants cause a feeling of euphoria that has been compared to the sensation of being drunk. Effects may include slurred speech, loss of **inhibition,** and impaired coordination. Inhalant users can experience serious negative effects the first time they use the drug, or any time after. These include headache, vomiting, unconsciousness, heart and brain damage, and sudden death.

Drugs such as crack, cocaine, methamphetamine, LSD, ecstasy, and heroin are very powerful. Their effects are very intense. People using these drugs might become suddenly aggressive or very depressed. They may try to hurt themselves or others.

Long-term health effects

Using drugs recreationally even just one time is dangerous, but long-term drug use is even more dangerous. In addition, long-term use of most drugs results in addiction.

People who regularly smoke marijuana are likely to become depressed. They may lose interest in normal activities and may have trouble relating to other people. Heavy marijuana use has been shown to affect concentration and memory, making learning difficult. Some of these problems may not go away even if the person stops using marijuana.

The long-term effects of inhalants can include severe personality changes. A user could become angry, violent, or depressed. He or she may also feel anxious and have difficulty remembering things. Frequent use of inhalants may cause weight loss, muscle weakness, and organ damage.

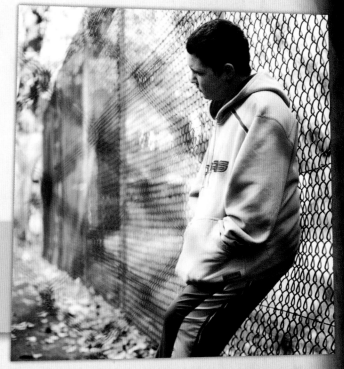

Using drugs can cause depression.

NEWSFLASH

A 2006 study found that heavy users of marijuana performed poorly on memory tests even when not using the drug. When asked to recall words from a list, frequent marijuana users could remember an average of only 7 words out of 15. People who did not use marijuana performed much better, averaging 12 words out of 15.

Case Study

Megan started using inhalants when she was 12. She stopped doing her schoolwork and started lashing out at other people. She even hit her mom. Megan got help and has been clean for two years, but she still has serious memory problems. Sometimes she forgets what she was talking about just a few seconds earlier.

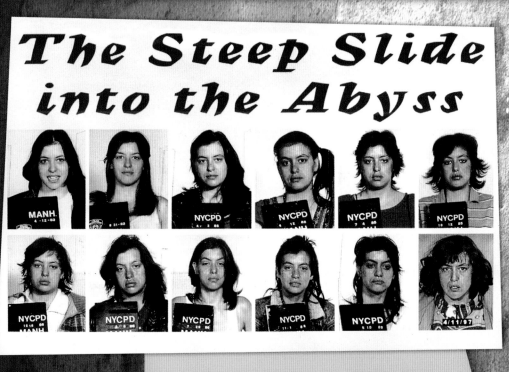

Drug use can change the way a person looks. These photos show the changes in one addict's appearance.

Other drug effects

The long-term effects of crack, cocaine, LSD, methamphetamine, heroin, and other drugs can be very serious. These drugs can cause permanent damage to the brain, the kidneys, liver, and other organs. People on drugs may not get the nutrients they need to stay healthy. They may develop wrinkles at a younger age than normal. Drug use can also lead to mental illnesses such as anxiety and paranoia.

It is easy to overdose on recreational drugs.

Drug dangers

Using drugs recreationally is dangerous for many reasons. Because every person's body chemistry is unique, some people may react badly to certain drugs. They may have **seizures,** heart failure, or be unable to breathe—and even die. There is no way to predict who will have a bad reaction.

The dosages of recreational drugs are not controlled by a doctor, so it is easy to overdose. Overdoses can result in brain damage or even death. In addition, people who overdose sometimes do not get medical attention because the people around them are also using drugs. Their judgment may be so impaired that they do not realize that their friend is in trouble. They may also not want to tell a doctor they have been using an illegal drug.

Case Study

Marissa was just 15 years old when she died from taking Ecstasy at a party. Although she had experimented with other drugs, she had not used Ecstasy before. Soon after taking the pill, Marissa's body went into **convulsions**, and her brain could not get the oxygen it needed. By the time Marissa arrived at the hospital, she was already brain dead.

Most drugs impair judgment and **motor skills.** Some drugs cause people to become depressed or violent. Crimes and accidents are often caused by people using drugs. Drugs that are injected pose an additional risk because people who inject illegal drugs often share needles. Sharing needles with other people can cause the spread of serious diseases such as hepatitis and HIV.

Mixing drugs

Since recreational drugs are not made legally, they could be mixed with other substances without users knowing. For example, they could be mixed with other drugs or dangerous chemicals. Mixing different recreational drugs can increase their effects, with dangerous consequences. Mixing drugs and alcohol is also dangerous. Many people have died from mixing drugs and alcohol.

A party can become dangerous if drugs are present.

Addicted to Drugs

Many drugs change the way the brain works so that the person becomes addicted to the drug. When the person does not get the drug, he or she feels strong **cravings** and will have intense **withdrawal** symptoms. It is very difficult for a person to stop using a drug once he or she has become addicted.

Drug use strains relationships and hurts families.

Top Tips

If you think a friend has a problem with drugs, you may be able to help by talking to him or her. Here are some tips:
- Talking about drugs can be difficult. You may want to talk to a trusted adult first.
- Choose a time when your friend is not using drugs.
- Do not accuse your friend of being an addict. Instead, say that you are concerned about his or her drug use.
- Say what you have seen him or her do when using drugs.
- Be prepared for **denial** and anger.
- Offer to help your friend get the help that he or she needs.

The life of an addict

An addict's whole life becomes focused around getting and using drugs. Since taking drugs is illegal and dangerous, many people lie about their drug use. Drug use among teenagers can make for stressful relationships with parents and friends. People who are addicted to drugs may become aggressive and lash out at the people around them. They can feel happy one moment and depressed the next.

Heavy drug users may have trouble doing normal daily activities, such as household chores. They may lose their jobs or fail in school. Drugs are expensive, and addicts may steal, beg, or sell drugs themselves to get enough money to buy drugs. People with serious drug problems may fail to eat properly, keep clean, or think of their safety. Some people become so addicted to drugs that they spend most of their time in a drug-induced stupor.

Some teenagers sell drugs to pay for their own drugs.

Recovery from Addiction

People who are addicted to drugs are often in denial. Family members or friends may need to help the person to understand that he or she has an addiction problem. Often, people realize that they have a serious problem only when their addiction leads to a crisis, such as being hospitalized or arrested. Young people who think they have a problem with drugs should talk to a parent, teacher, or other trusted adult.

There are many different kinds of treatment programs. No single treatment will work for everyone. Most people will benefit most from a combination of different approaches.

What do you think?

Some states are putting drug users who have committed crimes into treatment programs instead of jail. Supporters say that the programs help people turn their lives around and live productively. Opponents think that the new programs are soft on crime. Do you think people who abuse drugs should be sent to jail or to treatment?

Sometimes a person needs help to realize that he or she has a problem with drugs.

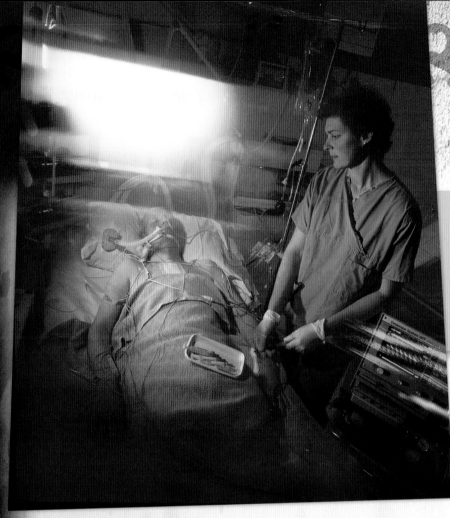

A crisis such as an overdose may make a person realize that he or she is addicted to drugs.

Detoxification

When drug addicts decide to stop taking drugs, they have to go through **detoxification** to rid their bodies of the drugs. During detoxification, an addict will experience withdrawal symptoms as his or her body adjusts to living without the drug. Withdrawal symptoms can be severe and may require hospitalization. People in detox may experience depression, anxiety, nausea, vomiting, headache, and even convulsions and hallucinations. In some cases, medications are given to help ease withdrawal symptoms and return the body to normal functioning.

Cravings can be very strong during this period. Addicts who are not hospitalized may have to be watched constantly to be sure that they are not finding ways to continue to use the drug. This period can take up to several weeks, depending on the drug and how heavily the person is addicted.

Rehabilitation

Programs for **rehabilitation** are an essential part of the treatment process. Rehabilitation helps recovering drug addicts by addressing emotional issues. It also teaches them new coping skills for staying away from drugs. Most people who do not participate in rehabilitation will relapse, or slip back into addiction. Some rehabilitation programs are designed especially for teenagers and young adults.

People who are heavily addicted to drugs over a long period of time often benefit from inpatient rehabilitation programs. Inpatient facilities are places where recovering addicts live for several weeks or months. The controlled environment keeps people away from drugs and temptation. At the same time, they learn new skills for living without drugs.

Case Study

At the age of 16, Darren was using OxyContin, heroin, marijuana, cocaine, and methamphetamine. He agreed to go to a rehabilitation program and soon realized that he would not be happy until he stopped using drugs. Darren worked hard to get clean. He made friends with some of the other guys in the group and got involved in helping other kids stay away from drugs.

Getting support is an important part of recovering from drug addiction.

Outpatient rehabilitation programs are effective for people who are not heavily addicted and who have strong family and community support. An outpatient facility is a place where recovering addicts go for treatment and support as they learn to live a drug-free life.

Long-term support

A support group or regular visits with a counselor or therapist help to keep a person from using drugs again. There are support groups especially for teenagers. Some counselors specialize in working with young people, too.

Unfortunately, even with the best care, some recovered addicts do relapse. When an addict relapses, he or she must begin treatment again. Although staying away from drugs is difficult, it can be done. Many people who have abused drugs in the past go on to live healthy and happy lives.

Real friends will never pressure you to try drugs.

Saying No

There are many different kinds of drugs, and it can be hard to say no when a friend offers them to you. But remember that using drugs recreationally is illegal and can be very dangerous. Here are some tips for keeping yourself safe:

- Stay away from situations where you know there will be drugs. Do not hang out with kids who you know do drugs, and stay away from unsupervised parties.

- Find a friend who is also committed to staying off drugs, and stick together. It is much easier to say no if you are not alone.

- Remember: It is okay to just say no; you do not have to give a reason.

- Stand up straight; use a strong voice and clear language.

Here are some different ways to say no, depending on your situation. Try to find a reason that is true for you:

"Not for me, thanks."

"No way, my parents will ground me for life if I get caught doing drugs."

"Coach will kick me off the team if I do drugs."

"I know someone who overdosed, so I never take drugs."

It is okay to be rude if someone will not stop pressuring you. Tell them to leave you alone or just walk away. Sometimes it helps to talk to someone you trust, such as your parents or guardians, an older sibling, teacher, or counselor. It can be hard to say no, but your real friends will respect your decision not to do drugs.

Prescription Drug Facts

Young people are abusing prescription and over-the-counter drugs today more than ever. Teenagers get the drugs from their own homes, from other kids, or even by ordering them from the Internet. Here are some facts you should know:

- Twenty percent of high-school students have abused prescription drugs.

- Children as young as 12 years old abuse prescription drugs.

- The most commonly abused prescription drugs are narcotics, depressants, and stimulants.

- Younger teenagers tend to abuse narcotics. The prescription drugs OxyContin and Vicodin can be just as addictive and dangerous as heroin.

- A dangerous new trend is "pharm parties." At these parties, teenagers pool whatever prescription drugs they have been able to round up and pass them around in bowls or baggies. Since the pills are unmarked, no one knows what kinds of drugs they are taking or how high the dosage is. People should never take unknown drugs.

- Twenty-five percent of all overdose-related emergency room visits are due to abuse of prescription drugs.

- Prescription drugs are not safer than illegal drugs. They can be just as addictive and just as dangerous.

Glossary

addictive causing the body to become dependent

anabolic steroid artificial hormone that causes the muscles and bones to grow

anxiety feeling of worry

coordination ability to move different parts of the body at the same time so that they work together

convulsion sudden, uncontrollable shaking or movement of the body

craving extremely strong desire

denial refusal to accept a truth

depressant substance that slows down the vital systems in the body

detoxification removing a poison from the body

euphoria feeling of intense happiness

flashback experiencing the effect of a hallucinogenic drug long after it has worn off

gateway drug drug that is not physically addicting, but may lead to the use of addictive drugs

glaucoma eye disease that can result in blindness

hallucination something seen or heard that is not really there

hallucinogen drug that causes people to hallucinate

illegal against the law

inhalant product with fumes that can be sniffed in order to get high

inhibition feeling of worry or embarrassment that keeps people from doing or saying whatever they want

marijuana dried leaves or flowers from the hemp plant

motor skill ability to use muscles effectively for movement

narcotic addictive drug that is used medically to reduce pain

overdose dangerously large dose of a drug

over-the-counter drug legal medicine that can be bought without a prescription

paranoia intense belief that other people want to harm you

peer pressure social pressure to behave or look a certain way in order to be accepted by a group

prescription drug medicine that can be legally obtained only with instructions from a doctor

rehabilitation return to a healthy condition and way of living

seizure sudden attack of a disease, especially convulsions

stimulant substance that speeds up the vital systems in the body

sudden sniffing death death due to heart failure that occurs within minutes of using an inhalant

withdrawal unpleasant physical and emotional symptoms that occur when a person gives up a substance on which he or she was dependent

Further Resources

Books

Amos, Janine. *Alex Does Drugs.* Cherrytree Books: London, 2003.

Kedge, Joanna, and Joanna Watson. *Drugs.* Chicago: Raintree, 2005.

Laliberte, Michelle. *Marijuana: A MyReportLinks.com book (Drugs).* Berkeley Heights, N.J.: Enslow, 2005.

Monroe, Judy. *Inhalant Drug Dangers.* Berkeley Heights, N.J.: Enslow, 2000.

Packer, Alex J., and Pamela Espeland. *Wise Highs: How to Thrill, Chill, & Get Away from It All Without Alcohol or Other Drugs.* Minneapolis, Minn.: Free Spirit Publishing, 2006.

Websites

Do It Now Foundation
www.doitnow.org

Get It Straight: The Facts about Drugs
www.dea.gov/pubs/straight/cover.htm

NIDA (National Institute on Drug Abuse) for Teens
teens.drugabuse.gov

Organizations

Drug Abuse Resistance Education (DARE)
P.O. Box 512090
Los Angeles, CA 90051-0090
Website: www.dare.com

Partnership for a Drug-Free America
405 Lexington Avenue, Suite 1601
New York, NY 10174-1699
Website: www.drugfree.org

Index